SOLDIER BALLADS and OTHER TALES

The Poems of W. D. Clarke
First Edition
2009

W. D. Clarke

Cover Photo: by Lucille Millarson
Millitary Memorabilia: courtesy of the New York
State Military Museum and Veterans Research Center
George A. Custer bust: by sculptor Ron Tunison
Western Memorabilia: courtesy of a private collector

SOLDIER BALLADS
and
OTHER TALES

Copyright © 2009 by W.D. Clarke

All rights reserved. No part of this book shall be reproduced or transmitted in any form or by any means, electronic, mechanical, magnetic, photographic including photocopying, recording or by any information storage and retrieval system, without prior written permission of the publisher. No patent liability is assumed with respect to the use of the information contained herein. Although every precaution has been taken in the preparation of this book, the publisher and author assume no responsibility for errors or omissions. Neither is any liability assumed for damages resulting from the use of the information contained herein.

ISBN 0-7414-5150-6

Published by:

1094 New DeHaven Street, Suite 100
West Conshohocken, PA 19428-2713
Info@buybooksontheweb.com
www.buybooksontheweb.com
Toll-free (877) BUY BOOK
Local Phone (610) 941-9999
Fax (610) 941-9959

Printed in the United States of America
Printed on Recycled Paper
Published December 2008

For

Those Whom

I Hold Dearly.

Acknowledgement

I would like to thank my dear friend and colleague Lucille Millarson for all the time she spent working with me on this project.

The many hours she put in typing, formatting, editing, changing, etc., without a single gripe was a Godsend.

Simply put, this book would not have become a reality without her timeless effort.

After all, it's not easy working with one of the world's biggest procrastinators.

Thank-you Lucille.

TABLE OF CONTENTS

1 / JOHNNY O

3 / DUSTOFF CREWS

5 / CHINOOKS

7 / FORGOTTEN VETERANS

9 / A DIFFERENT BREED

11 / HENRY LINCOLN JOHNSON

13 / THEIR LAST STAND

15 / LIBBIE CUSTER

17 / MYRTLE THE FERTILE TURTLE

19 / NORMANDY

21 / THE AMERICAN FARMER

23 / THE BOYS FROM TROY

25 / BILL JOHNSON'S TALE

27 / THE DEVIL AT THEIR DOOR

29 / THE NIGHT TIME ARMY

31 / THE NURSES

33 / THE PRIVATE AND THE MAJOR

35 / THE LUST FOR DUST

37 / THE LOACH MECHANICS LAMENT

39 / MILLARD'S FLAG

41 / Mc GOWAN'S

43 / THE K.P.

45 / TABACCA SPITTIN' SAL

47 / THE CIRCUMCISION

49 / THE PIRATE'S WIFE

51 / THE CHRISTIAN AND THE VIXEN

53 / SAND BAGGIN'

55 / THE LADY AND THE WHORE

57 / THE BALLAD OF PHARTZ LOUDER

59 / URCHINS

61 / THE OUTSIDER

63 / THE DEAD MARINE

65 / THE SPAN AM VET

67 / THE COMPANY SHIT BURNER

69 / THE PENNY PINCHIN' MAYOR

71 / GETTYSBURG

73 / THE VILLAGE ARMORY

75 / OL' DAD

77 / MILITARY VEHICLES

79 / CIGARS AN' WOMEN

81 / THE GUNFIGHT

83 / THE BIBLE THUMPER

85 / JIMMY THE BALL-TURRET GUNNER

87 / PRIVATE DOUGIE

91 / VETERANS

93 / EPILOGUE

JOHNNY O

My first poem, though it would be many years before I would write another. It was based on a Vietnam suicide and was written several years after I came home.

JOHNNY O

Johnny O, oh Johnny O, we didn't know him well,
We used to meet him now and then
on a path that led to hell.

Johnny O, oh Johnny O, he took himself a wife,
And then he traveled far away to live a soldier's life.

Johnny O, oh Johnny O, your wife's been out a cheatin',
Johnny O, oh Johnny O, you've taken quite a beatin'.

Johnny O, oh Johnny O, you got that awful letter,
We all tried to cheer you up and tried to make things better.

Johnny O, oh Johnny O, the shot gave us a start,
We wish you hadn't put that bullet through your heart.

Johnny O, oh Johnny O, we didn't know him well,
We used to meet him now and then
on a path that led to hell.

Johnny O, oh Johnny O, he died November seven,
Johnny O, oh Johnny O, we hope you're up in heaven.

DUSTOFF CREWS

*This poem was done as a tribute to
the DUSTOFF/ MEDEVAC crews of the
Vietnam War. It's based on a number of accounts told
by Veterans who witnessed first hand the risks
these brave crews took so others might live.
These men truly could "walk on water".*

DUSTOFF CREWS

The Air Cav brought us in, we hoped to God we'd win.
The enemy was stronger than we thought.

We tried to get dug in, dear God it was a sin
With dead and wounded lying all around us.

And during the attack, we called for Medevac
But it was just too hot, we were surrounded.

And then somebody cried, "I can't believe my eyes,
Look by God! Dustoffs coming in."

And then they hit the ground with confusion all around
With bullets ripping through the copter's skin.

They piled the wounded in, and then took off again
And before you knew it they were back for more.

And though some wounded died, many more survived
And yes, they owe their lives to these brave men.

For God gave them the courage, and it must be conveyed
Those crews went out and did this everyday.

Though many of them were slaughtered,
These men could walk on water.
God holds a special place for Dustoff Crews.

CHINOOKS

This pretty much covers what my helicopter unit did in Vietnam. Charlie rats stands for C-rations, Lord mounts are a spring loaded device that allows the drive shafts to flex, especially under heavy loads. Pressing On refers to our battalion's motto "PRESS ON".

CHINOOKS

We'd head out to the flight line,
before it was sunrise
And when the APU's were lit
these beasts would come alive.

The soft red glow of cabin lights
would give me quite a chill,
With thoughts of primordial dinosaurs
awaking on a hill.

These birds were big and dirty,
when run up they would scream
And then devour fuel, like fire on kerosene.

We flew all day from dawn till dusk,
and sometimes night time too
For wherever the artillery went, the chinooks
would be there too.

We slung the heavy 155's and yes the 105's too
And when it came to ammo, you bet we moved it too.

There was no glamour in our job,
our flightsuits were a mess.
Though sand and oil and fuel soaked,
this was our Sunday best.

And when it came to moving troops,
we'd load 'em up inside.
Then off to some far distant place,
we'd take 'em for a ride.

We flew into some hot LZ's, and carried wounded too
And when an aircraft was shot down,
we'd sling load that out too.

We bitched, we cursed, we pissed and moaned,
but this I have to say
Through all of this we loved our work,
I miss it to this day.

Some times were good, some times were bad,
and yes we lost friends too.
For wherever we were needed,
we were always there on cue.

Yes, flying was exciting, but with far too little pay
And yes we took some chances, with little time to pray.

We hauled huge loads of charlie-rats,
and yes we hauled beer too.
And for our friends in the infantry,
our hats went off to you.

We'd strain and lift and lift and strain,
we pulled some heavy loads
And if we weren't changing Lord mounts,
we were always on the go.

For those were times so long ago in far off Vietnam
And yet these birds still fly today in Iraq and Afghanistan.

And yes, there is a legacy for crews to carry on.
For old Chinooks will never die,
they just keep Pressing On.

FORGOTTEN VETERANS

But for the grace of God go I.

FORGOTTEN VETERANS

We see you come and go each day
As you pass you look away.

We see the disgust and contempt in your eyes
For those of us who are still alive.

We didn't intend to end up this way,
No matter what society may say.

We went away giving up our youth,
Perhaps too naïve for the bitter truth.

We weren't prepared for what we saw.
When they sent us to war
it was the luck of the draw.

And so we returned home,
thankful to be alive.
For many of our friends did not survive.

Though many of us weren't meant
to go back to school,
It didn't mean that we were fools.

All we wanted was a job, home and family.
What we got in return was society's damning.

Being turned away became the norm,
not the exception.
Perhaps we lacked your connection.

There was a time when we had dreams like you.
Within our ranks there are women too.

And for those of us, who have been alone,
Our biggest curse was coming home.

And for many of us, without much hope,
The drugs and the drink have helped us cope.

Yes, life's been a struggle just to survive,
With a weak spark of hope that's kept us alive.

So think of us, as you come and go each day,
As you pass and look away.

For we are still here,
your unwanted brethren.
Remember us lost and forgotten Veterans.

A DIFFERENT BREED

*I'm often asked if this poem is about me.
I plead the "fifth" but I will say however that
there just might be a little bit
of this character in everyone.*

A DIFFERENT BREED

There's a certain breed of character,
perhaps it's just their fate.
You know the type, you've heard it said,
"they were born five score too late".

While others march or take the lead,
they hear a different tune.
It's not a case of arrogance,
they have no silver spoon.

They never seem to find a place,
you can tell they don't fit in.
The heartbreak caused to family,
has been their only sin.

The restlessness inside of them,
is like a streak that's wild.
No matter how hard they try or are pushed,
they'll never be rank and file.

Their friends are few and of course it's true,
that life is too precious to squander.
Chasing treasure or gold until they grow old,
it's their curse and their fate to wander.

While others succeed, there's no use or need,
for routines that they find boring.
For their needs are so few and they'd rather make do.
It's their freedom those trapped find deploring.

When their lives are all done in a race that's half won
and there's no time left to ponder.
God will welcome them home to a new world to roam,
in that place that's way up yonder.

While it can't be denied that life's passed them by,
To outsiders their lives seem most ghastly.
Living life without plan, let society be damned,
They just did what 'ere made them happy.

HENRY LINCOLN JOHNSON

A tragic true tale about a WWI African American hero who "slipped right through the cracks".

HENRY LINCOLN JOHNSON

Henry Lincoln Johnson,
his death was quite a shame.
For by the time that Henry died,
few recalled his name.

He came back home from World War One,
to a ticker tape parade.
Yes, Henry he was honored
for the courage he displayed.

Henry was out of ammo,
as he threw his last grenade;
And although he was badly wounded,
his friend Needham he would save.

The enemy was upon them,
and began to drag Needham away.
They had a hold of Henry too,
it would be their unlucky day.

Then Henry grabbed his bolo knife,
for he was really riled.
He slashed and attacked the enemy platoon,
who ran like jackals in the wild.

Now Henry was a hero,
his wounds numbered more than twenty.
He received France's highest medal,
America didn't award him any.

Oh there were parades and honors,
when Henry made it back;
And like so many Veterans,
Henry slipped right through the cracks.

When Henry Johnson passed away
he was only thirty two;
And now there is a movement on,
for Henry to receive what's due.

For, Henry has many supporters,
who have taken up his fight.
They do believe this land of ours
will one day do what's right.

Inequality and prejudice
should never be ignored.
For what had happened to Henry,
must always be deplored.

And as the facts and records show,
there is nothing more to ponder.
The day will come when Henry receives,
The Congressional Medal Of Honor.

(June 25th 1876)
THEIR LAST STAND

*This one is about the Battle of Little Big Horn
or Battle of the Greasy Grass as the Lakota call it.
As a child I would often accompany my grandfather
to his favorite watering hole and gaze mesmerized
at the old Anheuser Busch print of "Custer's Last Fight"
as I drank my ginger ale.*

(June 25th 1876)
THEIR LAST STAND

Its peaceful now, the battle past
As the wind sweeps over the Greasy Grass.

While Troopers rode to Garryowen
The Indian ranks were rapidly growin'.

Their sacred land claimed by a nations right,
They had no choice but to fight.

With hollow promises and broken treaties
The soldiers came and burned their tepees.

But with all of his guns and troops and bluster,
It would not be enough for George A. Custer.

Benteen and Reno too far away
With their own dead and dying on that horrible day.

And so upon that grassy land
Custer and his men had made their stand.

And for Crazy Horse's Cheyenne and Chief Gall's Sioux,
In many ways it was their last stand too.

The sound of gunfire on that day
The war cries of Warriors on their way.

Almost half of the Sevenths lives were through.
Among the dead a black Trooper too.

And now if it's quiet with the wind lightly blowin',
They say if you listen, you'll hear Garryowen.

While Troopers and Indians now silently pass
As the wind sweeps over the Greasy Grass.

LIBBIE CUSTER

An amazing woman, she never remarried after her husband's death. She remained ever so dedicated to his memory until her dying day. I truly do hope she is, "resting with the man she married."

LIBBIE CUSTER

Libbie Bacon Custer, she was the Colonel's wife,
But after his misfortune, she lived a widows' life.
The Colonel he was lucky, to marry such a beauty,
A woman who would stand by him
during hostile frontier duty.

And when the worst did happen,
with he and his men dead,
The Army hurriedly, buried the bodies,
so riddled with arrows and lead.
And they sent the widows packing,
back to families or parts unknown,
As it wouldn't be proper for women,
to be unescorted or on their own.

Libbie went home to Michigan,
and with passion she did write,
And those who spoke out against her husband,
were in for one hell of a fight.
The Army disinterred the Colonel,
a body they thought his for sure,
And they reburied him at West Point,
where controversy has endured.

Libbie never remarried,
she remained faithful until her dying day.
She wrote three books on the exploits,
of her martyr who was valiant and brave.
Then at the age of ninety one,
away her life death carried.
I truly hope dear Libbie,
is resting with the man she married.

MYRTLE THE FERTILE TURTLE

This piece is based on a true story about an 8th Air Force bomber crew. I took some poetic liberty with the title. Myrtle was their original plane though they actually disappeared on a bomber called Judith Lynn. Their story was relayed to me by the bomber's wounded navigator Ken Carlson. Aircraft and crew disappearances back then were an all too common occurrence.

MYRTLE THE FERTILE TURTLE

Myrtle The Fertile Turtle,
it wasn't a sexy name.
Although it seemed to fit her,
this big ungainly dame;

And to the boys who loved her,
so far away from home;
And to all still carried as missing,
I dedicate this poem.

Myrtle was based in England,
back in World War Two;
And if you haven't guessed by now,
this grand old lady flew.

She was a battered B-24
and not just another crate;
She belonged to Bomb Group 93,
part of the "Mighty Eighth."

They'd take off on a mission,
with scores of other planes;
And as they approached their targets,
some went down in flames.

And when it came to Myrtle's turn,
on course she had to hold;
With flak exploding around her,
she did what she was told.

The searing metal pierced her sides,
as she dropped her deadly eggs;
And though she shook and shuddered,
for mercy she never begged.

And for her and those who escaped hells wrath,
to their bases they would return,
And during their mission debriefing,
the fate of their brothers they would learn.

It was on such a mission,
the Navigator nearly lost an arm;
The piece of flak that hit him,
would be his lucky charm.

And as he lay in a hospital bed,
his flying career at an end;
The pilot came by to visit him,
and say so long to his old friend.

For on the next day's mission,
the Navigator soon would learn;
That Myrtle and her crew,
were among those who did not return.

And so like many others,
who never made it home;
Their fate remains a mystery,
their cause of death unknown.

Whatever happened to them,
no one can really say;
Except that Myrtle and her crew
are missing to this day.

NORMANDY

*I've actually stood upon her rocky cliffs
as I imagined my father and his comrades
coming ashore.*

NORMANDY

I've stood upon your rocky cliffs,
As I scanned the sea for imaginary ships.
I've walked upon your hallowed ground,
Long gone now are your battle sounds.
      Normandy

The water slaps against your weathered shores,
Just as it did so many years before.
But now it doesn't run red anymore;
From all those battered bodies.

Your air now pure with the smell of the sea,
Gone is the smoke from the burning debris.
The scene of much suffering and misery.
Will man ever learn from what he has seen?
      Normandy

The bullets, the bombs, the wounded, the slain.
The sand on your beaches will always be stained.
The row upon row of endless crosses,
Barely begin to tell of the losses.

Oh what have you done to deserve such a fate?
The sorrow you witnessed the tragedy and hate.
The widows and children who whisper your name,
Old warriors returning, reliving the pain,
As they search for their friends among the white crosses.
You alone bore witness to all that it cost us;
And I pray that you won't see such horror again,
as your winds and your waves continue to rip.
When we speak thy name
it will linger forever on our lips.
      Normandy

THE AMERICAN FARMER

*Keeping America's population fed,
not to mention the military that literally
does travel on its stomach, the farmer's work
is never done. This piece was inspired by
the life of the late Ed Swartz Jr. and his family.
Ed was truly the epitome of the American farmer.*

THE AMERICAN FARMER

Remember the American farmer,
his work is never done.
He never stands by idly,
he's always on the run.
There's corn to plant,
there's cows to milk,
there's equipment that needs mending.
You wonder how he does it,
his work is never ending.

The farmer is up and working,
while the rest of us still sleep;
And this includes his family,
oh the hours that they keep.
They're always in a field,
with no time to unwind.
For the farmer and his family
aren't paid for overtime.

Some farms are small and simple,
some farms are more complex.
We can't afford to lose one,
they deserve utmost respect.
We never really think about
the wheat that's just been planted.
The food we eat, the milk we drink,
we've taken it for granted.

A farmer's lot isn't an easy one,
it's been that way for generations;
With disappointments in Mother Nature
and her lack of cooperation.
On top of this there are bills to pay,
the latest loan is pending.
He faces every challenge,
with fortitude unbending.

Oh the farmer's life is a busy one,
it seems his fate is sealed.
It's a challenge to feed America
and her military in the field.
So remember him and his family,
and their courage and dedication.
Our friend the American farmer,
the backbone of our nation.

THE BOYS FROM TROY

*It has been an honor and a privilege
to have known several of these Vets.*

THE BOYS FROM TROY

Most of 'em are gone now,
they've been leavin' us one by one;
That Second World War generation,
their time on earth now done.

There was a time, not so long ago,
when they were young like me and you;
When their hopes and dreams were put on hold,
at the start of World War Two.

They came from a National Guard unit,
one spilling over with pride;
For Troy, New York was their home town,
where life ebbed and flowed like the tide.

They were all part of one big family,
whose visions of excitement and adventure swirled.
Their rough and tumble battle cry was,
"South Troy against the World."

Their exploits have now become legend,
so many of them rest now in graves;
For many of them freely laid down their lives,
for their brothers whom they would save.

They were joined by others just like 'em,
from every single state.
Their nation called and they answered,
for freedom was at stake.

They were all part of the 27th,
a division now known far and wide.
In places like Makin and Saipan,
too many of these young men died.

Congrssional Medals Of Honor,
are awarded to so very few;
And for O'Brien and Baker and Salomon,
it was the only one that would do.

Today's men and women in uniform,
carry on that tradition you see.
Yes, the 27th is still alive and well,
for freedom has never been free.

Now the few of them ol' boys still livin',
stand with pride when Ol' Glory's unfurled;
And they still smile wide when they hear that ol' cry,
"South Troy against the World."

BILL JOHNSON'S TALE

*A gold rush inspired poem.
The Sleepy little town of Downieville California
is one of my favorite places.*

BILL JOHNSON'S TALE

Bill Johnson was a preacher, he's buried on yonder hill.
He never found himself a wife, I doubt now that he will.
He told me once a tale, I suspect it mostly true.
About a town that changed his life, I'll pass it on to you.

There was a time when he was bad, as bad as one could be.
He gambled and he swindled, a con artist that was he.
He moved about the minin' camps in search of easy gold.
And robbery wasn't beneath him, Bill Johnson he was bold.

The pickins' they were easy, as far as he could see.
For that's the way he lived his life in Californiee.
Indeed it was a wondrous life, he did just as he pleased.
And all of his ill gotten gains, he kept in an old valise.

One night he heard some rumors, so it was time to leave.
He knew that if he didn't, they'd hang him from a tree.
By moonlight he would travel, by daylight he would sleep.
He thought he had escaped the mob,
but upon him they did creep.

Suddenly they jumped him, and stabbed him in his sleep.
They kicked and punched and beat him,
then took his old valise.
They took his battered body and rolled it down a hill.
For sure he had expired, for half his blood was spilled.

It wasn't till the evenin' that Bill Johnson did come to.
By then he was a hurtin', for he was almost killed.
He crawled, he walked, he stumbled,
then slid down one big hill.
And as he lay beneath the stars,
he spoke this final will.

"Dear God I've been a sinner, I've done the devil's will,
But if you will but spare me, I swear I'll pay my bill."
His thoughts began to wander as he drifted off to sleep.
He awoke to a boney finger that poked him on the cheek.

"Am I in Hell" he whispered,
as he gazed at the stranger's face.
For now in the shimmerin' moonlight
his heart began to race.
The stranger reassured him, as he laughed in a loud shrill.
Relax my friend this isn't hell, you're just in Downieville.

Then in a bed they placed him,
for his wounds would need much tendin'.
They gave him a place behind the church,
for souls in need of mendin'.
He never forgot that minin' town,
or the folks who took him in.
And true to his word, he had given God,
he gave up his life of sin.

I've often traveled to this town, that had taken in old Bill.
At The Forks or The St. Charles,
I'd drink off the evenin' chill.
So if by chance you venture here, relax and drink your fill.
And remember that this isn't hell, you're just in
Downieville.

THE DEVIL AT THEIR DOOR

*A modern day "Tommy Atkins".
No matter how much time goes by,
some things never change.*

THE DEVIL AT THEIR DOOR

A soldier and his uniform
will always be fair game.
No matter how much time goes by,
it still remains the same.

In times of peace they'll mock it,
with comments none too subtle;
But listen how they'll change their tune
when their nation is in trouble.

For then they'll wave and praise him,
as they send him off to war;
Oh nobody likes a soldier
till the Devil's at their door.

"Support The Troops", "Freedom Isn't Free"
are the latest catch-phrase slogans.
But let them catch the scent of peace
and they'll boot him with their brogans.

But as long as there's a war on,
he'll get promotion and fair pay;
He'll go where he is ordered
and prepare for come what may.

While it's the fate of soldiers,
to jump through many hoops;
Be careful how you treat them,
they are not fools or dupes;

And you damn well should respect them
as they go to fight your war.
Oh nobody likes a soldier
till the Devil's at their door.

THE NIGHT TIME ARMY

It never ceases to amaze me
at the number of people who say it's their favorite.
Though somewhat disturbing to some,
it was written rather quickly
being based on recurring dreams.

THE NIGHT TIME ARMY

Sometimes when I lay down to sleep,
to get much needed rest.
Old friends come by to visit me
like uninvited guests.

They used to come occasionally,
but now most every night;
And though I'm glad to see them,
these visits don't seem right.

They creep into my dreams,
bringing friends who have died.
You never think to question,
how the dead can rise.

I find I'm back in uniform,
though my service was long ago.
There is no use to fight it,
you just go with the flow.

Sometimes these dreams bring happiness,
sometimes they turn to tears.
The one thing that they'll always do
is prey on all your fears.

These dreams will bring exhaustion,
for rest you'll seldom find.
You find it so amazing,
what stays fresh inside the mind.

I wonder if tonight I'll find the peace
for which I'm wishin'.
Or will they come and take me
on another senseless mission.

Whatever happens-happens,
but what is most alarming,
There's no escape or discharge
once you're in the Night Time Army.

THE NURSES

*One cannot say enough about
these Angels dressed in green.
Based on interviews with Veteran nurses,
many of them do suffer from post traumatic stress.
This poem also appears as THE CORPSMEN
in the book KOREAN WAR SKETCHES,
The Chosin Reservoir Campaign
by Steven Jordan and Anne Kelly Lane.*

THE NURSES

Here's to the Nurses,
they've been thru every war;
And for all that they have given,
you couldn't ask for more.

The aftermath of battles fought
to end a foe's oppression.
Believe me when I tell you
that there's no nobler profession.

The cries, the blood the casualties,
at times just wouldn't end;
The horrors that they witnessed,
the wounds that wouldn't mend.

The boys they saved, the boys they held,
as they saw life slip away;
It takes a special gift from God
to do this everyday.

And some of them were wounded too,
and some did pass away;
But through their dedication
many men are alive today.

So here's to the Nurses,
we owe our gratitude;
We couldn't begin to imagine
the hell that they've been through.

And yes, they too have nightmares
and post traumatic stress.
We owe them more than we can give,
they are our nation's best.

And some of them still suffer,
tending wounded in their dreams;
Still witnessing the horror, the blood,
the pain the screams;

So, here's to the Nurses,
there on the battle scene;
Here's to The Nurses,
God's Angels dressed in green.

THE PRIVATE AND THE MAJOR

*The age old taboo about fraternization
between officer and enlisted.
I like to think that Kipling would enjoy this one.*

THE PRIVATE AND THE MAJOR

I 'ad a chum from Liverpool, a Private just like me.
'E fell in love with a Major from The Womens Auxillary.

'E told 'er that 'e loved 'er, she said, "it couldn't be."

For it's rules and regulations
when you're in the King's Armee.
It's rules and regulations when you're in the King's Armee.

The Private 'e persisted, she was outside 'is caste.
She 'ad 'im at attention, as we stood there aghast.

Then all at once it 'it me, that it was all for show.
The Major 'id 'er feelings and, did not, want us to know.

The Army, they protested, of impropriety no one would tell.
They threatened a court martial, 'e said to, "go to 'ell."

So in a cell they threw 'im, then out of the King's Armee;
And now 'e doesn't 'ave to say, excuse or pardon me.

The Major 'e did marry, now it's legal as can be.

For it's rules and regulations
when you're in the King's Armee.
It's rules and regulations when you're in the Kings Armee.

THE LUST FOR DUST

The signature piece from a short series of California gold country inspired poems.

THE LUST FOR DUST

Gold can be addictive,
I've seen it cast its spell.
I've heard that Heaven's paved with it,
it's finding it that's Hell.

You'll break your back while driven on,
too dumb to accept defeat;
As you squat while swirling a gold pan,
with wet and frozen feet.

It's yellower than yellow,
this brightly colored dust;
And like a fallen woman,
to possess her men feel they must.

For sure, she will bring heartache,
I've seen her bring despair.
She often breeds misfortune, like most,
I've seen my share.

The anticipation makes you wander,
with those you shouldn't trust.
Eventually they'll turn on you,
as soon as things go bust.

But all this doesn't matter,
for it's lust that drives you on.
You're sure you're going to strike it big,
you've fallen for the con.

Now Mother Nature's got you,
Lord knows she can be cruel.
If you think she'll lead you to her gold,
you're just another fool.

And once you've found a nugget,
a clinker in your pan;
The hardships now seem worthwhile,
even part of God's master plan.

I've known my share of dreamers,
I suppose I am one too.
And yes, some found a fortune
but they number very few.

For most are down-n-outers,
whose dreams will not come true.
So listen to my warning,
what this lust for dust will do.

It will take you from your family,
it becomes your next of kin.
You'll spend your life and money
on a game you cannot win.

For gold is a seductress,
she'll seduce you if she can.
Don't let yourself be blinded
by all that glitters in your pan.

THE LOACH MECHANIC'S LAMENT

This little ditty is from a National Guard aero-scout platoon initiation, inducting the mechanics into the platoon. Needless to say, it didn't go over very well with the "Deltas".

(To the tune of Home on the Range)
THE LOACH MECHANIC'S LAMENT

Oh give us a wrench and a Loach* that's all bent,
And we'll make it all shiny and new.

But when we work with the Deltas**
who just fly and take showers,
Then there's hours of shit work to do,
Yes, there's hours of shit work to do.

So to all of the Deltas (Blank) you,
Yes, to all of the Deltas (Blank) you.

* Light Observation Helicopter
**67D Cavalry Scout

MILLARD'S FLAG

*The true story of Millard Orsini and the flag
he secretly made in a Japanese POW camp.
The flag is proudly displayed at
The Home Front Café in Altamont New York.*

MILLARD'S FLAG

It isn't very pretty and some may think it crude.
With old and faded colors of red and white and blue.

Oh yes there is a story. A tale that is true.
For Millard was a soldier with dreams like me and you.

His country called and Millard went. Our nation was at war.
He went to many places he'd never seen before.

The war raged on and on and on.
The Philippines had fallen.
With many dead or badly hurt, they took an awful maulin'.

His friends and he were marched away as Prisoners of War.
Their treatment was horrendous and death was at their door.

Their captors they were brutal, and some did not survive.
For Millard to see the land he loved he had to stay alive.

In secret Millard toiled, and hid what he had made.
To take the chances that he took, he truly was quite brave.

And when his work was finished, their hopes began to rise.
For when they gazed upon his flag
their dreams were kept alive.

Then all at once the word was out, the war was finally won;
As Millard held his flag up high,
our Air Force made a low and searching run.

Millard and his friends went home, to freedom that is true.
For Millard and his friends, had dreams like me and you.

Though Millard and his friends, have long since passed away,
Because of what they sacrificed, his flag still lives today.

So when you look at Millard's flag of red and white and blue,
Remember what it meant to them and what it means to you.

Mc GOWAN'S

A poem loosely based on those fondly remembered trips to one of Grandpa's favorite drinking establishments.

Mc GOWAN'S

In town there was a tavern,
where Grandpa liked to drink.
McGowan was the owner and also the bar-keep.
I used to go there with him,
when I was just a child.
It was a few blocks down the street,
about a quarter of a mile.

The place was always jumping,
how those old boys loved to drink.
I'd have a ginger ale,
with a cherry that turned it pink.
My Grandpa liked his whiskey,
dear Lord could that man drink;
And then I'd have to steer him home,
where Grandma'd raise a stink.

"Veterans and drunks", she'd holler
"Veterans and drunks".
"The only ones that hang out there
are Veterans and drunks".

They used to tell some tales there
and swore a lot there too.
They loved to rib each other,
that's what old Veterans do.
Oh, McGowan's was a lively place
where everyone had fun.
I didn't know it at the time,
those Vets were Span Am and World War One.

Though I was just a lad of five,
I reveled in their glory.
Although I really was too young
to appreciate their stories.
And Grandpa spun some tales too,
as he belted down a rye.
The smoke inside there was so thick,
it always burned my eyes.

And now too many years have passed,
since those treasured days.
I often think about them,
whenever I pass that way.
For McGowan's and its patrons
have long since disappeared;
And with them all their stories,
the good times and the cheer.
Sometimes I'll stop and reminisce,
at this lot now strewn with junk.
Dear Lord how I miss Grandpa
and those "Veterans and drunks".

THE K.P.

My first of many forays into the fine art of "Kitchen Police" duty. A painfully true tale.

THE K.P.

They lined us up at 2 A.M. to put us on K.P.
The Sergeant screamed an' yelled an' barked,
his cold stare fell on me.

Now I'll admit I weren't the best, at Army formality.
I wasn't shaved, my boots weren't bloused,
I was now his enemy.

The Sergeant looked me up n' down
and' soon began to scream.
"I'm givin' you the worst of jobs,"
that sergeant he was mean.

The temperature was 10 below,
when out the door I went.
Those garbage cans were full of slop,
they'd soon be my lament.

My job it was to scrub em' clean,
after dumpin' out the slop.
The problem was I wasn't told,
there was a dumpster 'round the block.

In front of me there was a grate,
I guessed it was a sewer.
It was there I dumped the garbage cans,
as my hands kept turnin' bluer.

The water from the hose froze quick,
as soon as it hit the cans.
While in the middle of this slippery mess,
I had all I could do to stand.

It wasn't long I dare to say,
inside there was a problem.
The drains were plugged an' they backed up,
the smell was pretty rotten.

They didn't know what caused the plug,
inside it was a mess.
Immediately I figured it out,
though I weren't about to confess.

That day was long an' towards the end,
they called for a "rotor rooter".
Thank God we left before they learned,
I was the sewer an' drain polluter.

TABACCA SPITTIN' SAL

*I've known a gal or two
who liked a good chaw now and then.*

TABACCA SPITTIN' SAL

Tabacca Spittin' Sal, Lord there weren't no finer gal.
She could shoot an' she could rope,
'cross the prairie' we would lope.

She preferred her life fast an' loose,
always spittin' tabacca juice.
That tabacca stained smile was infectious,
all the way to Hells Half Acre, Texas.

I expected she'd make a fine wife an' mother,
tho' she weren't none too gentle under the
covers. Whenever I tried to steal me a kiss,
it was generally just hit or miss.

Sometimes she'd smile an' then she'd spit,
or she'd just pucker an' make it quick.
As summer sunsets turned to red 'neath the stars
she'd make our bed.

I finally got up the courage an' spoke my mind,
but she said she weren't the marryin' kind.
It weren't long after we parted ways,
oh how I miss her cross-eyed gaze.

Each night I thank the stars that we crossed paths,
Lord I miss our monthly baths.
Her skin was like leather, with a complexion that was fair,
she had the most beautiful auburn hair.

She got herself killed in a barroom fight,
You know I still think of her each night.
She sure could slice you with her wit,
but oh dear God could that gal spit.

THE CIRCUMCISION

*I did take a few liberties on this one
though it basically is a true tale told to me
by a Veteran who experienced this first hand. Ouch!*

THE CIRCUMCISION

One day I was in uniform
waiting for Claudette.
This gentleman he sits next to me
and bums a cigarette.

He tells me he's a veteran,
a vet of World War Two,
And then he tells this story,
which he swore was true.

"In France we fought without regard
for hygiene or sanitation,
And whenever we could get a bath,
it was cause for celebration.

And then one day I was called up,
my records scrutinized,
and with a group of other men,
we learned we would be circumcised.

I kicked and punched
and screamed and yelled,
I tried to cut and run,
And when I felt the needles' prick,
the dirty job was done.

They wheeled me to another room,
where I would recover,
And when I looked beneath the sheet,
my private parts were plundered.

The pain was bad it really hurt,
it took a month to heal,
And if I dared to think of sex,
the thought would make me squeal."

I really felt uncomfortable
to hear this awful tale,
To do this to a serviceman,
they should have gone to jail.

And when the war had ended,
he went home to a grateful nation.
And for the missing part of him,
he received no compensation.

Then at last he had to go,
his train had just arrived,
And as he left he winked and said,
"I hope you're circumcised".

THE PIRATE'S WIFE

*A fun tale of piracy on the high seas.
The captain of the ship isn't necessarily
the captain of the home.*

THE PIRATE'S WIFE

I sailed for the King an' 'is Navy,
an' for the land I called 'ome,
An' when at last I 'ad me fill, I struck out on me own.

I served 'em as a Privateer, but for payment
I 'ad to barter,
An' when I 'ad me belly full,
I flew the Jolly Roger.

We sailed the routes of merchant ships,
an' took what we could plunder,
But when we hit the Caribbean,
a woman pulled me under.

We'd drink an' laugh an' play love's game.
me sea bag full 'o booty.
Since life was sweet an' life was grand,
I married this Jamaican beauty.

I promised 'er I'd never leave,
'er love was sweet like honey,
An' since we all was livin' high,
we was runnin' low on money.

So alas I 'ad to bid farewell,
for duty is always duty.
I promised I'd be back 'ome soon,
with 'a shipload full 'o booty.

We traveled North from port to port,
the wind was in our sails.
An' when it came to boardin' ships
our luck 'ad never failed.

An' while we was in a far North port,
I met a Norwegian beauty,
An' from 'ere to there or there to 'ere,
she always stayed close to me.

An' then the King was on our tail,
'twas time to 'ead for 'ome.
So to the Caribbean back we went,
for their women me men 'ad moaned.

An' so I came 'ome to me wife
with the treasures I 'ad found,
An' when she saw me new found friend,
with a fry pan I was crowned.

Me 'ead it hurt when I came to,
I still was seein' stars,
An' me friend was told to leave,
or else be boiled in tar.

A'las me rovin' days are gone,
as it's always fetch an carry,
For now she guards me day an night,
like a virgin would 'er cherri.
An' it's arrah to this an arrah to that,
or arrah to what 'er I say,
an' when me mates come callin',
she sends 'em on their way.

Oh 'ow I miss them days gone by,
as the terror 'o the sea,
An' now I'm doin' 'ousework,
or what 'er I can do to please.

It ain't so bad it could be worse,
I don't mind extra duty.
You see it is me lot in life for marryin'
this Jamaican beauty.

An so me friends I've chores to do,
I musn't dwell or tarry.
So listen when I tell ye lads,
"be careful who ye marry."

THE CHRISTIAN AND THE VIXEN

This poem is based on the true tale of a lad in the Merchant Marine during World War Two.

THE CHRISTIAN AND THE VIXEN

There was a lad from Brooklyn, a sailor he would be,
For all he ever wanted was to sail the seven seas.

His family they protested, although they were true blue,
And before I forget to mention it, he was a Christian too.

His messmates were an awful lot, hard drinking and depraved,
And though they always teased him, for their salvation he did pray.

It wasn't long I dare to say, that he began to stray,
He soon began to swear and curse, and have a drink each day.

And though this new behavior brought acceptance from the crew,
The thing that they found puzzling was, he read the bible too.

And then at last they came to port, for long awaited leave,
Of course the thing they wanted most, was some good debauchery.

They headed for the Casbah, for they had just been paid,
And our young friend from Brooklyn, for guidance he had prayed.

So in they went into a place with women to adore,
And if they wanted to spend some time, it cost them twenty more.

Then one by one they went upstairs with those whom they were smitten,
And our young friend from Brooklyn, he chose the Casbah Vixen.

Her beauty was exquisite, she had equipment too,
And yielding to temptation, is what the devil would have him do.

She beckoned him upon her bed inside the dim lit room,
He slowly started to undress, he was a blushing groom.

Oh yes she was alluring, with soft inviting thighs,
It was then that he discovered, his thing just wouldn't rise.

She didn't really seem to mind, though he felt quite deprived.
No matter what he did or thought, it wouldn't come alive.

And then at last his time was up and it was time to leave,
And all that he could think about was how his mates would tease.

And when they all were back on board, the ship went under way,
The laughter and the teasing just wouldn't go away.

It only took a day or two, but things began to change,
For all of his tormentors, were stricken with awful pain.

They moaned and winced and cried out loud, in pain and agony,
The problem they were having was, it burned when they went pee.

His mates they all were quarantined because of their condition.
He really felt relieved, he didn't have their affliction.

His mates were pumped with penicillin shots
to combat the awful infection.
It was an awful price to pay for sexual indiscretion.

And then it seemed all would be well, they'd join their fellow crew,
But then as fate would have it, they came down with scabies too.

And though the lad from Brooklyn would visit them each day,
For them it wasn't easy, in shame they'd turn away.

It really hurt to see his mates in such an awful condition.
But then at last he smiled and said,
"Thank Gawd I am a Christian".

SAND BAGGIN'

The job of filling sandbags in a war zone is a job that's never done. Overzealous sergeants take heed, lest you too may end up being bagged.

(To the tune of Camptown Races)
SAND BAGGIN'

We filled them bags both day and night,
Doo-dah! Doo-dah!
The job ain't worth a widows mite,
Oh, doo-dah day!

Fillin' bags all day, fillin' half the night,
If we can fill enough of them we'll get some sleep tonight.

The sergeant was an awful man,
Doo-dah! Doo-dah!
That's why he ended up in Nam,
Oh, doo-dah day!

Fillin' bags all night, fillin' half the day,
If we can bag enough of it, this place will go away.

The sergeant got into a fight,
Doo-dah! Doo-dah!
He did this almost every night,
Oh, doo-dah day!

Fillin' bags all day, fillin' half the night,
He made us fill a hundred more, just because of spite.

We finally had enough of him,
Doo-dah! Doo-dah!
And so we put an end to him,
Oh, doo-dah day!

Fillin' bags all day, fillin' bags all night,
We finally did get rid of him,
he put up quite a fight.

There ain't much more for us to say,
Doo-dah! Doo-dah!
And now it's time for us to play,
Oh doo-dah day!

Drinkin' half the night, sleepin' half the day,
Tomorrow there'll be more to fill, bet your (Blanking) A.

THE LADY AND THE WHORE

*Though the title may cause some to cringe,
this poem is really just a parable.*

THE LADY AND THE WHORE

I'll tell you lads a story and if you're smart you'll heed,
For when it comes to women, experience you'll need.

I know what you are thinking, you've heard it all before,
But listen to my tale of the lady and the whore.

There was a time when I was young, a soldier I was too.
And when it came to women, I loved myself a few.

Our lieutenant was a handsome man,
a soldier through and through.
He had himself a lady, he thought her love was true.

She always was available when he came into town,
But when he was out soldiering, she always played around.

There was an awful accident, our poor lieutenant died,
And all of us who knew him, we all broke down and cried.

(There was a fancy funeral the army did provide.)
His lady never shed a tear, a new man by her side.

And yes we soldiers miss him, I'll speak of her no more.
So listen when I tell you, that lady was a whore.

Our sergeant was a terror, and rough as an old cob,
But when it came to women, he was a gentle slob.

He was no dandy that's for sure, I dare not say much more.
Except our dear old sergeant, married himself a whore.

She really wasn't beautiful, attractive though for sure.
I know she really loved him, our sergeant he was poor.

And then one day it happened, the sergeant passed away.
His wife she couldn't take it, she cried and cried all day.

(There was a fancy funeral the army did provide.)
She held her head up proudly, we stood there by her side.

And yes we soldiers miss him, at times he made us crazy.
And may I say respectfully, that whore she was a lady.

THE BALLAD OF PHARTZ LOUDER

*Though the setting for this poem
is during the California Gold Rush era,
"Phartz" is loosely based on a character
I encountered back in my mining days.*

THE BALLAD OF PHARTZ LOUDER

Ol' Phartz, he was a miner, who hailed from New Orleans.
He came west to California, the land of gold and dreams.
I was sluicin' on the Yuba, just south of Downieville,
    When along came this ol' feller,
    who looked older than the hills.

    Now I've seen my share of characters
    while hangin' round the camps.
    The down-n-outs, the near-do-wells,
    the scoundrels and the scamps.
I eyed him very closely, my hand restin' on my gun.
    Should I go ahead and shoot him,
    or just make him turn an' run?

    I'd never shot nobody,
    though there were times I'd seen it done.
I started feelin' sorry for this broken down ol' bum.
    He stood there and he smiled
    as he stuck out his weathered hand;
An' after he introduced himself, I began to understand.

He was on his way to Downieville to pick up fresh supplies.
    I didn't fully trust him, as most miners do tell lies.
    I couldn't wait to see him go,
    an' I know this may sound crass,
But this ol' piece of buzzard bait continually vented gas.

About a half year later, I went to work at one of the mines;
An' there he was a workin', cuttin' timbers made of pine.
Whenever it was chow time, he was always first in line.
He'd always go off by himself, which suited us just fine.

I've never been standoffish, an' I wouldn't say I'm mean,
But this old' son of a mountain goat,
would eat nothin' but pork-n-beans.
It was pork-n-beans for breakfast, then pork-n-beans for lunch;
An' when it came to supper, he would eat what he ate at lunch.

Whenever he sat down to eat, he ate like he was famished;
An' because of his peculiar diet,
from the bunk house he'd been banished.
He'd hole up in a lean-to on the other side of camp.
It was where they stored explosives,
a fittin' place for this ol' tramp.

Eventually I left the mine, I preferred to work alone.
The solitude agreed with me, the Yuba was my home.
Occasionally I'd see ol' Phartz, with his mule and his gear;
An' when I heard he passed away, I confess I shed no tears.

He'd usually be a squattin', eatin' beans cold from the can.
Occasionally he'd warm 'em in a rusty ol' gold pan.
I wonder if those pork-n-beans were what finally did him in.
There wasn't much he left behind, he had no next of kin.

His boots and clothes were full of holes,
so none of 'em were taken;
An' I doubt no one would have wanted to see,
that ol' scavenger stark naked.
So they rounded up a Padre, to perform a funeral mass.
Then they covered him up right quickly,
as he still was ventin' gas.

Yes, I've seen my share of characters movin' up
and down the line.
The drunkards and the swindlers,
who would rob a widow blind.
But this I'll say with certainty,
to the nostrils none were fouler;
An' I hope to God, he broke the mold,
when they laid to rest Phartz Louder.

URCHINS

You will always see them by the roadside,
no matter where the war.
A truly sad reminder of mans inhumanity.

URCHINS

You see them by the roadside, no matter where the war;
The young the maimed the orphaned,
these casualties of war;

They'll gather round about you, shoeless with dirty faces;
An ever present reminder of
how inhumanity has disgraced us.

You wonder what the reason, for there to be such hate;
You dare not think about it, for them it is their fate.

But if you've got a conscience, indeed of them you'll think;
To see what life has dealt them, will make the sober drink.

There's times that you will curse them,
as beggars and as thieves;
For whatever isn't nailed down,
they'll take as they damned well please.

You can't hold it against them, for what else can they do;
Their background doesn't matter,
be it Christian, Muslin or Jew.

You see how they've adapted, such an enterprising lot;
It doesn't seem to matter what they have or haven't got.

You'll do what you can to help them,
then send them on their way;
And hope to God you've done your best,
to get them through the day.

It isn't fair to judge them, lest some day you'll be judged;
For doing what you couldn't do,
or not doing what you could've done.

THE OUTSIDER

Ah, to be in a town just lounging around just knowing that you'll never blend in. We've all been there.

THE OUTSIDER

Do you know what it's like to be in a town,
where nobody there knows your name?

You're just there for a rest, an anonymous guest,
with surroundings that seem so inane.

You will never blend in, unless you are kin,
And lo to you if you are not.

But you don't give a damn and you haven't a plan.
You accept it as part of your lot.

For it can't get no worse, it's just part of the curse;
Oh the life of a soldier is lonely.

When your friends are all dead, it's the living you dread;
And you'd welcome a gal who is homely.

Oh to be in a town and just lounging around,
You wouldn't think you'd miss being a soldier.

Now you're ready to fold, Lord the nights are so cold;
But dear God all the women are colder.

THE DEAD MARINE

A sad tale about a Marine who died tragically while home on leave after basic training.

THE DEAD MARINE

There was a death here in the States,
in a small but affluent town.
And even after all these years,
differing opinions still abound.

A young Marine while home on leave,
was stomped into the ground.
And after it was over,
no one had stuck around.

Some will say they're guilty,
some will say they're not.
And others will stay out of it
as the argument gets hot.

The altercation happened,
with name calling and a punch.
And what exactly happened next,
most will have their hunch.

For when it all was over,
and this can't be ignored;
An ambulance had not been called,
and the Marine, he lived no more.

For this small town it was a shock,
a case of pathos mixed with rumors.
The police investigation hampered,
by perfectly legal maneuvers.

And so the ones who stood accused,
were advised not to answer questions.
It also would be true to say,
there was not one confession.

For counsel they could afford the best,
having money has its perks.
And whether or not one likes it,
it's how our system works.

Because there were no witnesses
at the end of the confrontation;
There were no charges filed,
and all sides sued for compensation.

There was a civil trial,
the charge was wrongful death.
The defendants were found innocent,
the Marine's family received not a cent.

For after a night of drinking,
alcohol combined with a toke,
The jury had determined,
his own death he provoked.

And so it doesn't matter,
what side of the fence you're on;
No matter what the evidence shows,
opinions will abound.

But this I'll say for certain,
and I'm sure all will agree.
It always is a tragedy
to lose a young Marine.

THE SPAN AM VET

Sadly, all of them are long gone now.

THE SPAN AM VET

The obituary said he was a Span Am Vet.
After so many years I think of him yet.

We used to see, him walking each day.
Sometimes he would rest and watch us play.

He would sit on a bench absorbing the sun;
While we would be running and having fun.

At times he found it hard to stand.
I felt so sorry for this old man.

Sometimes we all would walk him home.
For this old man was all alone.

His wife had died at eighty two.
He had a son but he died too.

He smiled as he reminisced,
about his wife and his son.
I guess that's how it is
when you're ninety one.

He patiently waited for his time to be done;
While we would be running and having fun.

Then on a rainy autumn day,
when it was too wet to go out and play.
That poor old man he passed away,
his time was up he couldn't stay.

The obituary said he was a Span Am Vet.
After so many years I think of him yet.

THE COMPANY SHIT BURNER

*This poem is about one of the "unsung"
heroes of the Vietnam War.
Though tongue in cheek, it always brings a smile
to anyone who served in Vietnam
or in any primitive part of the world
where indoor plumbing wasn't available.*

THE COMPANY SHIT BURNER

I've traveled all around the world
and I've seen some awful places,
And often do I think about
some old and special faces.

For when I traveled long ago
to participate in war,
I met a special soldier,
our company adored.

He had no rank or power,
not in the usual way,
But when he spoke they listened,
as they backed away.

His job was so important,
he took it all in stride.
He tended the latrines you see,
a task he did with pride.

It truly was a nasty job,
a job that had no beauty.
Because of what he had to do,
he had no other duties.

And while we marched and sweated,
and labored in full kit,
I never really envied him,
his job was burning shit.

He mixed his gas and diesel,
he'd make a chemist proud,
For when he lit his mixture,
it made the blackest cloud.

The smell was overpowering,
the kind you can't forget,
And ever since I smelled it,
I still can smell it yet.

You couldn't be around him,
the stench was in his hide,
And though we really liked him,
he was often ostracized.

But those were times so long ago
and times today ain't changed,
For in the lands where plumbing ain't,
the job remains the same.

So if you meet him on the street,
this proud and old sojourner,
Let's raise a glass and shake the hand
of the company shit burner.

THE PENNY PINCHIN' MAYOR

A playful poke at the budgetary worries of the small town mayor.

THE PENNY PINCHIN' MAYOR

The fire she was a spreadin'
when they sounded the alarm.
One pumper truck was broken,
the other at a burning farm.

There was a truck to do the job,
but damn, it wouldn't start.
The Mayor vetoed new equipment,
he had a miser's heart.

Well now he was beside himself,
it was his house that was burnin'.
He cursed and yelled but to no avail,
the old boy he was fumin'.

The firemen, they did show up,
as the Mayor screamed his indignation.
Alas it wasn't a total loss,
they saved the rock foundation.

GETTYSBURG

*Brother against brother, friend against friend,
this horrific battle was considered
the turning point of the Civil War.*

GETTYSBURG

She once was a peaceful industrial town
with a laid back attitude.
Until two Titan armies clashed,
destroying all solitude.
The battle raged on for three long days,
one of history's most brutal.
As brother against brother
and friend against friend fought,
for beliefs they deemed not futile.

Her hills and her fields,
her woods and her streams,
once echoed with the sound
of cannon and screams.
The lingering stench of death and gangrene,
The living, disfigured from wounds so obscene.
Spilled blood and young corpses
now part of the land,
Can we truly appreciate
the respect she commands?

The long forgotten heartbreak
of those left behind,
Who would never again see,
those for whom they had pined.
And now people dress in period clothing,
attempting to capture the pomp and the glory.
Long gone are the men who lived the real story,
for what they had witnessed was horrible and gory.
Yes, gone are the veterans who came year after year;
To this land of much blood shed, and so many tears.

A landscape torn open and wounded,
where hot steel and lead once poured;
Now monuments abound here,
like pawns on an old chessboard.
So many feet have trampled now,
upon her hallowed ground;
And like a smitten suitor,
her admirers keep coming around.

But above all,
we'll honor and remember,
all of those who died.
The soldiers who were sacrificed,
on the winning and losing side;
And it seems that her long lines of tourists,
are a courtship that never will cease.
Oh Gettysburg, it is thy lot,
to never rest in peace.

THE VILLAGE ARMORY

An alarming number of these "bastions of the community" are being lost largely under the guise of progress and the cost involved to adequately maintain them.

THE VILLAGE ARMORY

The armory in the village,
I heard its coming down.
They say it has no purpose,
it's old and falling down.
It's just an ancient building,
that has outlived its use.
The stone and brick and mortar,
is cracked and coming loose.

That armory has stood there
for more than a hundred years;
And now they want to raze it
and make it disappear.
Oh what will they replace it with
after the wrecking ball?
Will there be another parking lot,
or super mini-mall?

It's here as a reminder
of freedom and of pride.
Where people came together,
when trouble was on the tide.
Its here our soldiers gathered,
before they went to war;
And some of them returned here
and some of them no more.

And what about the blood drives
and patriotic days;
And all the good that went on here
in long forgotten ways.
And is it not considered,
sacred and hallowed ground?
This bastion of the community,
now old and falling down.

Is it too late to save it,
will it be worth the time?
There always is a price to pay
when pride is on the line.
And when it comes to freedom,
it's always worth the cost.
We may just lose a piece of it
when an armory is lost.

OL' DAD

*When it came to stories,
Dad had a million of them.*

OL' DAD

Ol' Dad he was a veteran
and a teller of tales too.
Whenever I would question him
he'd swear they all were true.

My Mom would frown and roll her eyes,
for by heart she knew each verse;
And if she dared to 'spill the beans',
dear God would ol' Dad curse.

A friend of Dad's borrowed his old truss,
to avoid going into service;
And as he stood before the Doc,
he naturally became quite nervous.

The doctor stamped his form M.E.,
did this mean Medical Exemption?
Dad's friend could barely contain himself,
he believed in divine intervention.

The doctor said, "It means Middle East,
and I hope you do like mammals,
Anyone who'd wear a truss upside down,
can certainly ride a camel"

During a hospital stay in Bordeaux France,
when Dad was wounded severely,
A soldier who was just brought in,
was despondent and quite teary.

A nun came by for a quick 'look see',
and to her he said discreetly,
"If you had been hit where I was hit,
they would have missed you completely."

Yes, ol' Dad was a teller of tales,
while on a roll he'd never get tired.
His face would light up
and his eyes would shine,
like a firehouse dog at a fire.

And now his tale telling days are done,
and to give the devil his due,
He never told a soul but me,
what was false and what was true.

MILITARY VEHICLES

*They're uglier than sin, yet beautiful
in their own right. You truly couldn't begin
to count the times they've saved a soldier's hide.*

MILITARY VEHICLES

Vehicles in the military
do suffer from abuse.
It really doesn't matter
be they Jeep, Humvee or Deuce.

They never were designed you see,
to take out on a date.
They'll take you where you need to go,
though speed and ride ain't great.

Today they've gotten wider,
though still uglier than sin.
They really haven't changed that much,
when it comes to beauty they'll never win.

The gears still grind, the clutch is stiff,
the four wheel drive's the same.

It's amazing how they feel at home
in sand, mud, snow and rain.

The paint schemes are far from beautiful,
yet each vehicle is maintained with pride.
You couldn't begin to count the times,
they've saved a soldier's hide.

CIGARS AN' WOMEN

*I'm really far from an expert on both subjects though
I certainly know what I like.
Sometimes the two intertwine nicely,
just as long as neither one bites.*

CIGARS AN' WOMEN

I likes me cigars an' me women.
Lord knows that I've sampled a few.
A stogie can be satisfyin' ,
Like a woman that loves only you.

On each I am far from an expert,
But I certainly knows what I likes.
For one is a passionate woman,
The other a cigar that won't bite.

The size an' the shape doesn't matter.
Tho' I prefer me a long thin cheroot.
If you've got you the love of a woman,
Then her size an' her shape becomes moot.

While soldierin' down in Honduras,
It was there that I took me first smoke.
Oh the women down there have the darkest of hair,
An' they'll love you even when you're flat broke.

It was there that I met me a maiden.
She was older but I didn't care.
I was her young willin' stallion,
An' she was me unbridled mare.

She did have herself a strange habit,
One for which I didn't despair.
She would smoke a cigar in the evenin'.
(How the smoke hung so sweet in the air)

She would then become so wrought with passion,
While the beans on the back burner cooked.
Now I won't explain why, Lord she surely weren't shy.
Let's just say on cigars I got hooked.

Oh, I've been many places since then,
An' some memories are as gray as me hair.
The quality of cigars just like women,
Vary greatly from so-so to rare.

Now I sits in me creaky ol' rocker,
Blowin' blue smoke rings into the air.
Now it's just me an' some lingerin' memories,
An' I really have nary a care.

While I sits here just contemplatin',
Sometimes long into the night.
I dream of those days thru the blue smokey haze,
Of a woman an' cigars that won't bite.

THE GUNFIGHT

*The setting was Tombstone, Arizona
October 26, 1881. The most famous gunfight
in history pitted the Earp brothers and Doc Holliday
against the Clanton's and McLaury's.
This is a much scaled down version
of what happened on that fateful day.*

THE GUNFIGHT

Four men were on a mission
as they turned down Fremont Street.
Side by side they continued on,
town folk stared in disbelief.

One was Virg, the other Morg,
there was also Doc and Wyatt.
Sheriff Behan claimed
the culprits were disarmed,
the four men weren't going to buy it.

The Clanton's and McLaury's
had been spoiling for a fight.
Ike Clanton had gotten them all stirred up,
they would shoot the Earps on sight.

The O.K. Corral would be the place
for this final confrontation.
The stage was set the time was here;
"Throw up your hands,"
Virg thundered with indignation.

Then all at once all hell broke loose
and when all the shooting was done,
Billy Clanton and the McLaury's were dead.
Billy Claiborne and Ike had run.

Of the four men who had walked alone,
all had been shot except for Wyatt.
Amongst the carnage and the lookers on,
the scene was far from quiet.

These four men did survive the fight,
their would be killers were doomed to fail.
The dead were displayed in their Sunday best,
though heavily rouged they looked ghastly and pale.

THE BIBLE THUMPER

*This piece was inspired by a number
of stories I've heard concerning
the finding of religion under fire.*

THE BIBLE THUMPER

There's one in every unit, someone
that loves to preach.
No matter how you tempt him,
he's beyond the devil's reach.

He'll always thump the bible,
to the point you'll want to scream.
Though now I'm ashamed to say it
but to him we were awful mean.

For when he preached the bible,
we smoked and cursed and drank
And it was not beneath us,
to pull the worst of pranks.

But when you're in
the thick of things
and friends begin to die,
The fear of death and dying,
can make the strongest cry.

Now when it came to dying,
this thumper had no fear.
Although we thought him crazy,
he said his God was near.

And when the worst was over
and for those who walked away,
There was a new perspective
on this man who always prayed.

When the Chaplin came to visit us,
we lined up though in pews.
Although it took some time to change,
we changed our point of view.

It was just a few months later,
alas the thumper died.
We listened to the service
and stood there teary eyed.

Now, through the years
and time that's passed,
I've done some dreadful things.
Whenever I stop and think of him,
his voice still clearly rings.

Lord knows I'm far from perfect,
I still drink and smoke and curse.
It'll be that way till the day I die
and I'm whisked off in a hearse.

As I sit here postulating,
with my mouth half full of chew,
I'm glad to say in my humble way,
I thump the bible too.

JIMMY THE BALL-TURRET GUNNER

This poem is based on a tale told to me in 2008 by ninety year old Jimmy.

JIMMY THE BALL-TURRET GUNNER

Poor Jimmy he had a wee problem,
For he always had to go pee.

They made him the ball-turret gunner,
On a beat up old B-17.

He was stuffed down into the turret,
Like a fish inside a glass bowl.

It was there on his very first mission,
He had a problem with bladder control.

While up in the wild blue yonder,
You know it gets god awful cold.

Just imagine poor Jimmy's dilemma,
With the urine that he just couldn't hold.

There was a small tube in the turret
But with Jimmy it didn't quite reach.

Dear lord it's a terrible feeling,
When dryness and comfort's been breached.

They raised Jimmy up before landing,
At the end of an eight hour inning.

Now imagine the surprise of the crew,
When they saw Jimmy a splashing and swimming.

It was later that day in the evening,
Young Jimmy signed out on a pass.

Sitting there on the table before him,
Was a container that was made out of brass.

Now I think that I know what you're thinking,
About what Jimmy decided to do.

For Jimmy had an idea
And I think it just might surprise you.

Jimmy reached down inside of the container,
Then he pulled out a fist full of condoms.

It was right then and right there in that moment,
He found the solution to his urinary problems.

Now the next time that Jimmy went flying,
And according to Jimmy it's true.

He just peed inside of each condom,
And then knotted the ends of them too.

Young Jimmy was so dry and happy,
As he packed them in under his seat.

He then fired his guns at the on-coming Huns,
As he contributed to Germany's defeat.

PRIVATE DOUGIE

This tale is typical of many who were drafted into service whether they were ready or not. They rose to the occasion and did what they were expected to do, doing so with pride and honor.

PRIVATE DOUGIE

Dougie was in the Army,
though that was long ago.
He'd never been away from home,
and poor Dougie he was slow.
The Army had a quota then,
and Dougie fit the bill.
All they would require of him was,
to shoot and shoot to kill.

They sent him away to training camp,
that was quite aways down South.
The sergeant barked and yelled at him,
he had the foulest mouth.
Dougie was put on fire watch,
while everyone went into town.
Poor Dougie drifted off to sleep,
as each tent burned to the ground.

Now Dougie was in an awful fix,
and the sergeant threatened to shoot him.
The Army had enough of Dougie,
so they began proceedings to boot him.
So in the meantime while the others drilled,
they put him on K. P.
Though it was done as punishment,
he ate everything he could see.

The baker yelled, he needed sugar,
he had chocolate cake to make.
Now Dougie began to feel at home,
he loved it when his mother baked.
While Dougie filled the mixing bowls,
with the exact amount requested.
He decided he too would become a cook,
so the procedure he digested.

The soldiers lined up for their dessert,
as the baker beamed with pride.
And Dougie he was happy too,
in fact he almost cried.
Then all at once the jig was up,
the soldiers began to wretch.
They began to spit and curse and swear,
Dougie's neck everyone wanted to stretch.

Poor Dougie was beside himself,
he said it weren't his fault.
In school he never learned to read,
the bag's label actually said salt.
In Europe things were heating up,
Dougie's discharge was put on hold.
He found himself aboard a ship,
Dougie went where he was told.

He was loaded on a landing craft,
for the invasion into France.
If Dougie was going to redeem himself,
this would be his only chance.
Dougie hit the beach with everyone else,
to move forward was the Army's desire.
The deafening noise, the smoke and the death,
it was like a dragon breathing fire.

He came upon a platoon of men,
pinned down by a machine gun nest.
As he calmly rushed by, a group of them pleaded,
for Dougie to take cover and rest.
With all of his might he threw a grenade,
as bullets chewed up his ground.
The explosion took out the machine gunner's nest,
his ears rang from the deafening sound.

It was only an hour or two after that,
Dougie took a chunk of shrapnel to the head.
As his blood flowed red from the gaping hole.
Dougie was left among the dead.
But somehow fate had smiled on him,
it was discovered that he was alive.
By a hospital ship he went back to the States.
He was lucky to have even survived.

Dougie came home to the family farm,
in time he would find him a wife.
The experiences he went through way back then,
would forever be the highpoint of his life.
Now Dougie's been gone for a number of years,
the death of a Vet isn't anything new.
They went where they were told,
and they did so with pride,
that's how it was done back in World War Two.

(a poem for children)
VETERANS

*My one and only children's poem.
This was done for a Veterans Day program
at an elementary school in Troy, New York.*

(A Poem For Children)
VETERANS

Every family has one,
be they living now or dead.
Perhaps you've got their helmet,
which you've placed upon your head.

It could have been your father's,
who just came back from war.
Or maybe it was Grandpa's,
the one not around anymore.

Perhaps it belonged to Grandma,
a nurse in Vietnam.
Maybe it was your Uncle's,
the one whose name was Tom.

The thing they have in common is,
they all went off to war.
It was to protect our country,
and freedom forever more.

You see, they all are Veterans,
who answered their nation's call.
And many never made it home,
for our country they gave their all.

And so whenever you see one,
be it at home or in a parade,
Remember what they've done for us,
and the sacrifices they have made.

They all deserve a word of thanks,
for their service to our country and to you.
Perhaps one day the time will come,
when you'll be a Veteran too.

EPILOGUE

Some of my poems are mildly irreverent.

The Pirate's Wife, *The Christian and the Vixen*, *Circumcision*, and *The Ballad of Phartz Louder*, are a few examples.

I have on occasion used swear or curse words in my poems but generally I don't make a practice of it. *The Company Shit Burner* (which always brings a smile to Vietnam Veterans) is an example of this, as are *The Loach Mechanics Lament*, and *Sand Baggin*.

My poetry is rhyme based. It is uncomplicated and unpretentious. The poems are fairly easy to memorize if the reader is so disposed. Some are based on actual Veteran stories which are sometimes sad or disturbing, while others are humorous. A number of my poems were done strictly for fun, some of which were inspired by my travels out West.

If my poetry brings enjoyment or a smile to the reader's face, I have done my job.

W. D. Clarke

W. D. Clarke
Standing in the doorway of a
Chinook helicopter during monsoon season,
Camp Eagle, Vietnam.

1970